Al-Tariqa Burhaniyya-Dasuqiyyah-Shadhuliyya

Murshid
F . A . Ali ElSenossi

A Glimpse of Islam and its

Inner Teachings

Travel by the Power of *Hu*

A Glimpse of Islam and its Inner Teachings

By

Murshid F.A. Ali ElSenossi

Almiraj Sufi Press

Title

A Glimpse of Islam and its Inner Teachings

Author

Murshid F.A. Ali ElSenossi

Almiraj Sufi & Islamic Study Centre Inc.

www.almirajsuficentre.org.au

Publisher

Almiraj Sufi Press

Broken Hill, Australia

2025

ISBN

978-1-7636006-3-8

Contents

Introduction

Islam is a profoundly deep and meaningful way of life through which man is enabled to inject each moment of his earthly existence with harmony, balance, and a sense of the Sacred.

This book has been compiled as a sharp, penetrating glance at, and very basic introduction to, the Islamic Traditions, both outward and inward, and it aims at putting right several misconceptions about this Faith which persists today.

Each man and woman owes his or her own self to look carefully at this Final Revelation which God has sent to His creation, because it is within the Islamic Teachings that a human can discover his reason for being.

Mankind has been honoured above all the creation, for only Man has been created with the potential to know his Lord and therefore understand himself.

"He who knows himself, knows his Lord"
The Holy Prophet Muhammad ﷺ

For many people in the West, Sufism (*tasawwuf*) is an unknown quantity. If they have heard of it, it is probably in connection with one of the following: Sufi dancing, Sufi music, Sufi poetry, or Sufi stories.

While these practices are related to Sufism, they form only a very small part of the teaching. Many of the Western groups who practice them are not always aware of this fact. When searching for a group or teacher, one really should investigate thoroughly to ensure one connects to an authentic teacher who is truly connected to the life force that is Islam and Sufism.

بسم الله الرحمن الرحيم

The Continuity of the Message

Islam is the primordial religion. It is the Creator's final Revelation to mankind, and it encompasses the guidance and messages of all the previous Prophets and Messengers - from Adam to the seal of the Prophets, Muhammad ﷺ. Islam is the Message from Allah to His creation, in its final and perfect form.

قُولُوٓا۟ ءَامَنَّا بِٱللَّهِ وَمَآ أُنزِلَ إِلَيْنَا وَمَآ أُنزِلَ إِلَىٰٓ إِبْرَٰهِـۧمَ وَإِسْمَـٰعِيلَ وَإِسْحَـٰقَ وَيَعْقُوبَ وَٱلْأَسْبَاطِ وَمَآ أُوتِىَ مُوسَىٰ وَعِيسَىٰ وَمَآ أُوتِىَ ٱلنَّبِيُّونَ مِن رَّبِّهِمْ لَا نُفَرِّقُ بَيْنَ أَحَدٍ مِّنْهُمْ وَنَحْنُ لَهُۥ مُسْلِمُونَ

Say: We believe in Allah and that which was revealed to us and that which was revealed to Abraham and Ishmael and Isaac and Jacob and the Tribes and that which was given to

Moses and Jesus and to the prophets from their Lord: We make no distinction between any of them and to Him we submit

(Holy Qur'an 2:136)

All of the Prophets of Allah were in the state of utter submission to their Lord. All were Muslims, that is, those who submit themselves to God.

بسم الله الرحمن الرحيم

Islam and Muslims

The word Islam means both "peace" and "submission to the Will of God." Islam is a complete, spiritual way of life, with recommended codes of behaviour governing everything from the moment of conception (and before) to the time of death (and after), from the simplest thing such as tying your shoelaces to more complicated worldly matters such as business transactions and matters of inheritance.

A Muslim is someone who submits himself consciously to the Will of God, following the teaching of the Holy Qur'an and the *sunnah*, or personal practices and example, of the Holy Prophet Muhammad ﷺ. By following the teaching in the way the Holy Prophet Muhammad ﷺ practiced it upon his own self, we are given the means to purification of the self, thereby drawing nearer to Allah and earning His Love.

قُلْ إِن كُنتُمْ تُحِبُّونَ ٱللَّهَ فَٱتَّبِعُونِي يُحْبِبْكُمُ ٱللَّهُ

وَيَغْفِرْ لَكُمْ ذُنُوبَكُمْ وَٱللَّهُ غَفُورٌ رَّحِيمٌ

Say (Oh Prophet), if you do love Allah, follow me: Allah will love you and forgive you your sins, For Allah is Oft-Forgiving, Most Merciful

(Holy Qur'an 3:31)

For Muslims, God is identified by the Name "Allah." This Name is not used to identify any being other than the One, Most Glorious Creator of all. The basic teachings of Islam consist of five foundational pillars and six articles of faith.

The Five Pillars

In Islam, every action that is performed with the awareness that it fulfils the Will of Allah is an act of worship. However, there are specific acts of worship known as the Five Pillars, which form the very foundation and framework of the spiritual life of a Muslim.

The Testimony of Faith or *shahadah*. This is the declaration that "there is no God but one God and Muhammad is the slave and Messenger of God."

Prayers (*salat*). Muslims offer their prayers five times each day, before sunrise (*fajr*), at noontime (*dhuhr*), late afternoon (*'asr*), just after sunset (*maghreb*) and the night prayer before retiring (*'isha*). All Muslims face the *Ka'aba*, the House of Allah in Mecca, when offering their prayers.

Each of the five daily prayers are an opportunity for man to re-orient himself in the direction of his Lord. A sense of the Sacred is instilled in him as he leaves whatever worldly activities he is engaged in and turns towards his Creator in this supreme act of worship. It is highly important not to disturb someone who is in prayer as they are in a state of direct communication with their Lord. The Holy Prophet Muhammad ﷺ has said, "It is better to wait for 40 years and turn to ashes than to pass in front of a person in prayer" (*Sahih Bukhari*).

Fasting (*sawm*) during the month of *Ramadhan*. The Islamic fast is a complete fast. Outwardly, Muslims abstain from food, drink, smoking, and marital relations from approximately one hour before sunrise to just after sunset. Inwardly, he strives to abstain from anything that will distract him from Allah, even standing guard over his thoughts, not allowing negativity to take hold. Fasting is a powerful act of worship and, even though the entire community is engaged in the fast, it is an intensely personal form of devotion, which is purely between Allah and His slave.

The fast is compulsory upon all healthy, adult Muslims who are resident in their homes during the month. Those who are travelling or ill, pregnant, lactating, or menstruating are exempt from the fast. If a person is unable to complete the fast during the month of *Ramadhan*, the required number of days may be made up at any other time during the year.

Charity (*zakat*). A compulsory 2.5% levy is payable on all surplus wealth each year. Man is not alone in this world. He lives in society and is partly responsible for the wellbeing of his fellow man. Islam prescribes the annual payment as a way of keeping wealth in a state of movement, thus benefiting both the giver and the receiver.

The Pilgrimage (*hajj*). The pilgrimage to the House of Allah in Mecca and performance of the associated rites is compulsory upon all Muslims who are able - once in a lifetime. This is the return to the source of Islam.

بسم الله الرحمن الرحيم

The Articles of Faith

Muslims believe in Allah (God), His Books, His Messengers, His Angels, the Hereafter, and that everything, both good and bad, comes from Allah. Muslims believe in all 124,000 Prophets and Messengers of Allah, from Adam عليه السلام to Muhammad ﷺ and all those in between (peace be upon them all), making no distinction between them. All the Prophets of God are highly revered and respected in the teachings of Islam. The books of Allah include the Torah, the Bible, the Psalms of David and the final revelation to mankind, the Holy Qur'an. In Islam, those who follow the Jewish and Christian teachings are known as "the People of the Book."

لَّيْسَ ٱلْبِرَّ أَن تُوَلُّوا۟ وُجُوهَكُمْ قِبَلَ ٱلْمَشْرِقِ وَٱلْمَغْرِبِ وَلَٰكِنَّ ٱلْبِرَّ مَنْ ءَامَنَ بِٱللَّهِ وَٱلْيَوْمِ ٱلْءَاخِرِ وَٱلْمَلَٰئِكَةِ وَٱلْكِتَٰبِ وَٱلنَّبِيِّۧنَ وَءَاتَى ٱلْمَالَ عَلَىٰ حُبِّهِۦ ذَوِى

ٱلْقُرْبَىٰ وَٱلْيَتَـٰمَىٰ وَٱلْمَسَـٰكِينَ وَٱبْنَ ٱلسَّبِيلِ وَٱلسَّآئِلِينَ وَفِى ٱلرِّقَابِ وَأَقَامَ ٱلصَّلَوٰةَ وَءَاتَى ٱلزَّكَوٰةَ وَٱلْمُوفُونَ بِعَهْدِهِمْ إِذَا عَـٰهَدُوا۟ وَٱلصَّـٰبِرِينَ فِى ٱلْبَأْسَآءِ وَٱلضَّرَّآءِ وَحِينَ ٱلْبَأْسِ أُو۟لَـٰٓئِكَ ٱلَّذِينَ صَدَقُوا۟ وَأُو۟لَـٰٓئِكَ هُمُ ٱلْمُتَّقُونَ

It is not righteousness that ye turn your face towards East or West; but it is righteousness to believe in Allah and the Last Day and the Angels and the Book and the Messengers; to spend of your substance out of love for Him, for your kin, for orphans, for the needy, for the wayfarer, for those who ask and for the ransom of slaves; to be steadfast in prayer, to practise regular charity, to fulfil the contracts which ye have made and to be firm and patient in pain (or suffering) and adversity, and throughout all periods of panic. Such are the people of truth, the God fearing

(Holy Qur'an 2:177)

بسم الله الرحمن الرحيم

The Oneness of Allah

Allah is the One, the Truth, the Eternal, the Most Holy, the First, the Last, the Alive, the Self Subsisting. Islam enjoins faith in the Oneness and Sovereignty of Allah, which makes man aware of the significance of the Creation and everything within it. It also brings about the awareness in man of his own place in the Universe. When man sincerely believes in the Oneness of Allah, he is freed from all fears and superstitions because he is ever conscious of the Presence of Almighty Allah.

فَأَيْنَمَا تُوَلُّوا فَثَمَّ وَجْهُ ٱللَّهِ

Whithersoever ye turn, there is the Presence of Allah
(Holy Qur'an 2:115)

سَنُرِيهِمْ ءَايَٰتِنَا فِى ٱلْأَفَاقِ وَفِىٓ أَنفُسِهِمْ حَتَّىٰ يَتَبَيَّنَ لَهُمْ أَنَّهُ ٱلْحَقُّ

We shall show them Our signs upon the horizons and within themselves, until it becomes clear to them that this is the Truth

(Holy Qur'an 41:53)

and

وَنَحْنُ أَقْرَبُ إِلَيْهِ مِنْ حَبْلِ ٱلْوَرِيدِ

We are nearer to him than his jugular vein

(Holy Qur'an 50:16)

Faith alone is not enough – it must be confirmed by actions. A Muslim must endeavour to act upon and put into practice all that he learns from the Holy Qur'an and from the Holy Prophet Muhammad ﷺ. Knowledge that is not acted upon is only partial.

Humanity is looked upon as one family, with each member living under the Universal Omnipotence of the Creator and Nourisher of all – Allah. Each person must strive, with whatever means have been given to him, to help humanity.

بِسْمِ ٱللَّهِ ٱلرَّحْمَٰنِ ٱلرَّحِيمِ

قُلْ هُوَ ٱللَّهُ أَحَدٌ

ٱللَّهُ ٱلصَّمَدُ

لَمْ يَلِدْ وَلَمْ يُولَدْ

وَلَمْ يَكُن لَّهُۥ كُفُوًا أَحَدٌۢ

Say, He is Allah, The One and Only. Allah, The Eternal, The Uncaused Cause of all that exists, He begets not, nor is He begotten and there is nothing that can be compared unto Him (Holy Qur'an 112).

Man, the Free Agent

Man is the highest creation of Allah. He has been created with the highest potentialities; the greatest of which is the potential to "know" his Lord. Everything returns to Allah, but only humans come into the universe with such tremendous potential for growth and development – the capability to become a true human being.

$$\text{إِنَّا لِلَّهِ وَإِنَّا إِلَيْهِ رَٰجِعُونَ}$$

Verily to Allah we belong and verily unto Him we are
returning
(Holy Qur'an 2:156)

Man is left relatively free to choose his own way of return. He can follow the path laid down by one of the Prophets of Allah or he can follow his own caprices and whims. All roads lead back to Allah, and it is up to us in what condition we will meet our Lord and which of the many "Faces" of Allah we will encounter in that meeting.

Allah has shown man the true path of return. He has given us the Holy Qur'an and the perfect example of the Prophet Muhammad ﷺ. Man's success and salvation lie in following the right path. Every human has been given the choice – whether to follow the path that will lead him to darkness or the Straight Path, which will take him into the Light, fill him with Light and expand his consciousness.

ذَٰلِكَ ٱلْكِتَٰبُ لَا رَيْبَ فِيهِ هُدًى لِّلْمُتَّقِينَ

This is the Book; in it is guidance sure, without doubt, to those

who are conscious of Allah

(Holy Qur'an 2:2)

لَّقَدْ كَانَ لَكُمْ فِى رَسُولِ ٱللَّهِ أُسْوَةٌ حَسَنَةٌ لِّمَن كَانَ يَرْجُوا۟ ٱللَّهَ وَٱلْيَوْمَ ٱلْآخِرَ وَذَكَرَ ٱللَّهَ كَثِيرًا

*Ye have indeed in the Messenger of Allah a beautiful pattern
(of conduct) for anyone whose hope is in Allah and the Final
Day, and who engages much in the remembrance of Allah*

(Holy Qur'an 33:21)

The Holy Qur'an and *Ahadith*

The Holy Qur'an is the final Revelation from Allah to His creation and is the basic source of Islamic teachings and laws. It is the discernment between truth and error.

Over a period of 23 years, the Holy Qur'an was revealed to the Holy Prophet Muhammad ﷺ through the Archangel Gabriel عليه السلام, the Angel of Revelation. Contained within the Holy Qur'an are teachings of wisdom, worship, morality, knowledge, history, social justice, economics, politics, jurisprudence, and human relations.

The Holy Qur'an contains everything required by the human to enable him to live a noble and dignified life and to prepare himself for the next life. The message of the Holy Qur'an is timeless. The Teachings are perfectly applicable to all people, in any circumstances, in any era. It is not a historical document; it is a living Revelation.

While it is complete in its revelation, it is never ending in its openings of new understandings to mankind.

The Holy Prophet Muhammad ﷺ was of the highest and noblest character. He is described as "like the Qur'an, walking" (*Sahih Muslim*). *Ahadith* are the teachings, sayings, and actions of the Holy Prophet Muhammad ﷺ. They have been meticulously recorded, gathered, and transmitted through a chain of authentic authorities. These sayings and actions form the secondary source of the Islamic teaching. Through the Holy Prophet's ﷺ words and actions, the Holy Qur'an is further explained, and we are shown how to implement the teachings in our own lives by his example. To reach a deeper knowledge of the Qur'anic Message, it is necessary to live one's life in the closest possible way to that of the Holy Prophet ﷺ.

Worship

The Holy Qur'an says:

وَمَا خَلَقْتُ ٱلْجِنَّ وَٱلْإِنسَ إِلَّا لِيَعْبُدُونِ

I created jinn and men only to worship (know) Me
(Holy Qur'an 51:56)

Worship is the highest function of mankind. It is the reason why he was created – to "worship" or to "know" Allah. Islam gives to man the means to fulfil this highest of all functions. The Muslim is urged to constantly look within himself in an attempt to purify the intentions behind each thought, each word, and each action; then to think, speak, and act with total sincerity. Empty worship is mere ritualism which neither elevates a man nor enables him to fulfil his reason for being. In Islam, each thought, word, and action can become a form of worship, a means by which the Muslim can know his Lord and draw closer to Him.

The Islamic Way of Life

Islam is a totality. Within its supreme teachings are the guidelines by which all of humanity can live a meaningful life in this world. The transitory nature of this life is ever present in Islamic teachings and the Muslim is constantly being guided to his true goal – the Only Goal, which is Allah Almighty. This life is a precious gift. It is not to be squandered in frivolous, meaningless activities, but is to be lived with a sense of the Sacred and a view to the Hereafter.

In Islam, man is a unity, a whole. He is not a fragmented collection of separate parts. Through realisation of this unity, which he contains within himself, man is given the necessary indications to bring him to the knowledge of the Unity of Allah. The Holy Qur'an and the *ahadith* invite man to look on the horizons and within himself at the signs with which Allah Almighty has surrounded him, in order to awaken him to the Unity of Existence.

The Islamic Way of Life is a way of balance. The sacred and the secular are not separate parts of man and his life. Islam shows man how to inject every moment of his existence with the Sacred, thereby making every action and every word a means by which he can grow and develop into a true human being.

The Historical Perspective

The Holy Prophet Muhammad ﷺ is the Seal of the Prophets. He is the final Prophet of Allah, who has been sent to humanity with the Final Revelation in its perfection. He was born of a noble family in the year 570 AD in the sacred city of Mecca.

Since the time of the Prophet Abraham ﷺ, Mecca has been the centre of worship of the One God, Allah. With the passage of time, the purity of Mecca had become defiled by idol worship and disbelief. The moment had arrived when the last of Allah's Prophets would appear to cleanse the land of idolatry.

Just before the Holy Prophet ﷺ was born, his father, 'Abd Allah, died in nearby Yathrib (Medina) on his way home from a trading expedition. Soon afterward, his widowed mother, Aminah, became intensely aware of the light she was carrying within her womb – the Light of the Seal of the Prophets.

His ﷺ early years were spent in the desert with a foster family. This was the custom of the time, and the purity of desert life strengthened the sons of Meccan families. During this time, he was separated from his mother. However, when he was returned to Mecca, mother and son enjoyed a brief but happy interval together. When he was only six years old, his mother also passed away, leaving Muhammad ﷺ an orphan. His remaining childhood years were spent under the care and protection of first his grandfather, 'Abd al Muttalib, and then his uncle, Abu Talib.

The childhood, youth, and early manhood of the Holy Prophet ﷺ reveal the immensity of his nature – his perfection, his purity, his generosity, trustworthiness, and his overflowing spirituality. Throughout these years he was being prepared by Allah Almighty to receive the Revelation, which initially descended upon him in his fortieth year, during the month of *Ramadhan*.

$$\text{اقْرَأْ بِٱسْمِ رَبِّكَ ٱلَّذِى خَلَقَ}$$

$$\text{خَلَقَ ٱلْإِنسَـٰنَ مِنْ عَلَقٍ}$$

Read! In the Name of thy Lord and Cherisher, Who created –

created man out of a (mere) clot of congealed blood"

(Holy Qur'an 96:1-2 – The First Revelation)

Initially, knowledge of the Qur'anic revelation was confined to the family and closest friends of the Holy Prophet ﷺ. In time, Allah Almighty commanded him to openly proclaim the Holy Qur'an. Years of persecution and hardships followed, as the unbelievers of Mecca and the surrounding cities desperately, and in vain, attempted to put an end to the Pure Message of the Oneness of Allah.

$$\text{يُرِيدُونَ لِيُطْفِئُواْ نُورَ ٱللَّهِ بِأَفْوَٰهِهِمْ وَٱللَّهُ مُتِمُّ نُورِهِۦ وَلَوْ}$$

$$\text{كَرِهَ ٱلْكَـٰفِرُونَ}$$

Their intention is to extinguish God's Light with their mouths,

but Allah will complete (the revelation of) His Light, even

though the unbelievers may detest it

(Holy Qur'an 61:8)

After many years of persecution, the Holy Prophet Muhammad ﷺ and his followers made their migration (*hijra*) to another Arabian oasis city called Medina. Revelation continued to descend, and the message of Islam continued to spread throughout Arabia and beyond. After years of struggle and patience, Mecca was conquered and the Holy Ka'aba was cleansed of idols as Islam entered the hearts of the unbelievers. Once again, Mecca was returned to being the Pure Centre of the Religion of the Oneness of Allah.

Revelation of the Holy Qur'an continued over a period of 23 years. During the Holy Prophet's ﷺ Farewell Pilgrimage to Mecca, the final Islamic Revelation descended:

ٱلْيَوْمَ أَكْمَلْتُ لَكُمْ دِينَكُمْ وَأَتْمَمْتُ عَلَيْكُمْ نِعْمَتِي

وَرَضِيتُ لَكُمُ ٱلْإِسْلَٰمَ دِينًا

This day have I perfected your religion for you, completed My favour upon you and have chosen for you Islam as your religion

(Holy Qur'an 5:3)

At the age of 63, the Holy Prophet Muhammad ﷺ passed from earthly life and was put to rest in the blessed city of Medina, the City of Light.

Misconceptions About Islam

With the advent of modern technology, more and more information is available to us about the world's peoples and faiths. While so many barriers to religious and cultural understanding have been broken down as a result of this, there are still some misconceptions and misunderstandings where the religion of Islam is concerned.

To clear these misconceptions, it is essential the teachings be investigated at their source, not through the misguided interpretations of those outside the circle of Islam. It is also important to differentiate between what is "Islamic" practice and what is "cultural" practice among Muslims. As occurs within all faiths, not every Muslim is a good example to observe or emulate. The main areas of misinformation seem to be concerning the status of women in the Islamic society, marriage and divorce, and the concept of *jihad* (Holy War).

The Status of Women

Islam's original precept is equality between men and women, as indicated by their equal responsibility before Allah on the Day of Judgement, when the scales of deeds are set. Islam recognises that all people, male or female, have a responsibility towards themselves, to their families, and to the community at large. Each person is responsible for fulfilling his or her own role to the best of their ability.

Unlike western women, the Muslim woman did not have to struggle to gain equality, respect, dignity, and honour. These natural rights were freely granted to her with the descent of the Islamic Revelation over 1400 years ago. Before Islam spread through the Arabian Peninsula, the Arab woman, like her sisters in other lands, lived in a world of oppression, subservience, and inequality. The Sacred Law revolutionised her existence. Her life, her property, and her honour were protected. Islam granted her equal rights to earn her own money, own her own property and to contract her own business arrangements.

Under Islamic law all women have the right to choose their own husband, retain their family name and identity, and to request a divorce if it becomes necessary to do so. The Holy Qur'an also clearly states the laws of inheritance for both men and women, protecting their wealth and property from misuse.

Chastity is paramount within Islam and, ideally, should emanate from within men and women, not through the imposition of closed doors and veils. Both sexes are taught to be modest in their dress and in their behaviour, always bearing in mind that they are within the sight of Allah Almighty.

Marriage and Divorce

Islam's original precept is the continuity of the relationship between husband and wife. Marriage is a sacred contract and should ideally bring about the spiritual development of both partners. However, it is recognised that as humans, we make mistakes and sometimes things go wrong. In such circumstances, it is preferable to negotiate a divorce rather than continue to live an unhappy marital life, stifling the development of both partners.

Holy War (*Jihad*)

Islam's original view is that of individual freedom. A person is free unless it is shown, by their words and actions, that he or she is unable to properly discharge the responsibility of such freedom. If injustice, oppression, and idolatry become firmly established within a society and aggression towards Allah and His people becomes manifest, then something must be done to restore the balance of the society.

In the early times of Islam, the people went out to fight against the aggression and hostility of those who tried to extinguish the Light of Islam. Upon returning from one such expedition, the Holy Prophet Muhammad ﷺ said to those who were with him, "We have returned from the lesser *jihad* to the greater *jihad*" (*Kanz al-Ummal*). When questioned about the meaning of this "greater *jihad*," he replied, "The greatest enemy of man is that which resides between his two sides." Waging war against the desires and whims of the lower self and bringing it to a state of true submission to the Will of Allah is the real Holy War.

For those who are successful in bringing this "inner war" to an end, there is peace, joy, tranquillity, and knowledge of Allah. When a person becomes awake and enlightened, the light and vibration that emanates from them will also affect the people around them, bringing more peace and more light.

Wake up people, return to your Lord, follow His Guidance and His way, follow in the footsteps of His beloved Prophet, Muhammad ﷺ and take up the spiritual inheritance that is truly yours. Be part of the solution, not part of the problem.

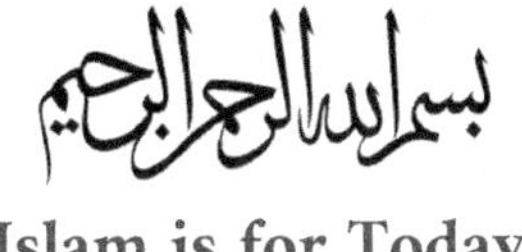

Islam is for Today

Islam's Rational Appeal

In our era, when man's worldly knowledge is rapidly growing, he is truly in need of a sense of the Sacred if he is to be prevented from falling into irrecoverable error. Islam is for today, for this very moment. Islam can give to modern man the balance that has been lost during this desperate pursuit of outer knowledge. Man's every day activities can be regularly infused with prayer, contemplation, and good deeds, all of which will remind him of the transitory nature of the earthly life. His inner activity and his outer activity can be brought together and become balanced, making him into a whole man.

Islam has tremendous appeal to any sincere seeker of knowledge. Islam has the unique ability to bring into balance the inner and outer dimensions of existence. Humans live according to their view (or picture) of life.

The tragedy of secular societies is that they fail to connect the scientific and the spiritual, the outer and the inner, the secular and the religious. Islam brings harmony. Within Islam, the human is able to develop into a true human being.

The Brotherhood of Man

Islam can put an end to mutual rivalry, hatred, and racism. In the Sight of Allah, all His creations are equal, and His Mercy extends to everything, living or inanimate. When Islam is practiced with sincerity and love of Allah, man is enabled to understand his own smallness in the face of the Greatness of Allah. When man comes to truly believe that Allah is the Greatest, his eyes are opened to the fact that every human is as much in need of the Mercy of Allah as he is himself. Every man is his brother, every woman his sister, as they gather under the Infinite Protection of their Creator.

The Family

Respect for all life is a basic Islamic teaching as every created thing bears witness to the Creator. Within the Muslim family this quality of mutual respect is strong and vital. Not only do the young respect the old, but likewise, the old respect the young. Always, there is a balance to be found as each member of the family respects and honours the rights of each of the other members. Mutual assistance, love, and generosity bring about equilibrium and create an atmosphere that is conducive to the spiritual growth and development of the individual and the family unit as a whole.

Tasawwuf – The Inner Teachings of Islam

In all human societies there are certain men and women whose very nature demands more than just faith in God. From within, these people feel the yearning and hear the irrepressible call towards knowledge of God. If they respond to this interior call, then the pursuit of this goal will become the reason for their being. *Tasawwuf* is the heart teaching of Islam. With everything there is an outward and an inward, a body and a heart, the Law and the Way.

The Islamic science called *tasawwuf* is more commonly known as Sufism in the Western world. *Tasawwuf* is the science that holds the key with which a human can unlock the very secrets of existence, opening into the One Real Existence, which is Allah.

Tasawwuf is the study and practice of the very essence of Islam. The traveller on this path places himself totally under the supervision and guidance of his Spiritual Master or *Murshid*. Here is where the deeper meanings of the Islamic Teachings are studied and contemplated upon and put into practice. The Holy Qur'an and the *ahadith* are the Pure Sources of *tasawwuf* and only under the direction of a true Spiritual Master is one given the means to penetrate the richness and beauty of the Inner teachings of Islam.

Knowledge of the Absolute, of Allah, is for those few who turn themselves totally towards the true goal. Yet, the sweetness of *tasawwuf* is there for everyone to taste. Everyone can be refreshed, even if it is only by being sprayed with a fine mist of cool water on the outer edge of the clear flowing fountain of Islamic spirituality – which is *tasawwuf*.

Tasawwuf is the method by which one can purify the heart and make one's surrender (Islam) total so that God will take up His residence within, for as He says, "Neither My heavens nor My earth contain Me, but the heart of My true slave contains Me." To be a true slave is the struggle of the spiritual work within *tasawwuf*.

All true Sufis are Muslims but not all Muslims are Sufis. Those who follow the Sufi Path or Way practice both the outer and the inner teachings of the Holy Prophet Muhammad ﷺ.

Shari'ah is the Islamic Law. It is the method that Muslims use to transform their base qualities such as envy, hatred, and lust to noble qualities such as generosity, love, and compassion. It is a code of conduct which assists the Muslim to perfect the externals of his life by bringing his beliefs and actions into line with the Islamic teaching.

For Muslims in general, *shari'ah* is the code of conduct, which, if they follow, will guarantee them a place in Paradise when they die. For the Sufi, *shari'ah* is the foundation upon which to build their spiritual lives. They concern themselves not only with purifying their actions but take it further by purifying their thoughts and intentions as well. So, *tasawwuf* is the inner aspect of the *shari'ah* by which the Muslim purifies his heart through rectifying his inward (or esoteric) acts.

Shaykh Maseeh Ullah Khan, in *Shari'ah and Tasawwuf*, states,

"Tasawwuf in fact is the *ruh* (soul) and state of perfection of the *deen* (Islam). Its function is to purify the *batin* (inward) of man from the lowly bestial attributes of lust, calamities of the tongue, anger, malice, jealousy, love of the world, love of fame, stinginess, greed, ostentation, vanity, deception, etc. At the same time it (*tasawwuf*) aims at the adornment of the heart with the lofty attributes of repentance, perseverance, gratefulness, fear of Allah, hope, abstention, Unity, trust, love, sincerity, truth, meditation, reckoning, contemplation, etc. In this way, attention towards Allah Most High is inculcated in man. This is in fact the purpose of life. *Tasawwuf* is therefore not at all negatory of the *deen* and *shari'ah*. On the contrary, it is incumbent for every Muslim to become a Sufi. Minus *tasawwuf*, a Muslim cannot truly be described as a perfect Muslim."

It wasn't always the case that *shari'ah* and *tasawwuf* were taught separately. In the time of the Holy Prophet ﷺ, both exoteric and esoteric Islamic instructions were given in the gatherings of the Holy Prophet ﷺ. It was only later when Islam had spread to many countries throughout the world and the Caliphate was divided into separate political and religious jurisdictions that scholars formulated the teachings of Islam into separate entities. Because of this separation, some Muslims are unaware that *tasawwuf* is an integral part of the Holy Prophet's ﷺ teaching and so they regard it as blasphemous or innovative. Muslims who hold this belief are encouraged to speak with a Sufi Shaykh who will be able to demonstrate to them that the teachings of *tasawwuf* are to be found in the Qur'an, the *hadith*, and the *sunnah*.

How the Sufi uses the exoteric aspects of Islam as a means to esoteric knowledge

In the Holy Qur'an, in *Sura al-Qaf*, Allah says He is closer to us than our jugular vein and the science of *tasawwuf* is the means to draw as near to Allah as He is to us.

Shaykh Muzaffer says in his book *Love is the Wine*, "You have to make certain efforts and bear certain pains. God is nearer to you than you are to yourself. God has said,

'There are seventy thousand veils between you and Me, but there are no veils between Me and you'.

"God says I am closer to you than your jugular vein. God is that close to you – within you and completely surrounding you. Everything around you is God. You cannot see God unless God chooses to be visible to you. And God will become known to you in a way that is different from the experience of anybody else. So, you will never be able to convey fully your experience to another. God Most High, Who does not fit into all the earths and heavens, has found a place in the heart of a believer. The experience of God comes from your heart. God will appear to you according to your potential, according to your capacity. It is different for each of us."

The method for doing this is *tasawwuf,* the Islamic spiritual psychological study of the Self and Knowledge of Divinity. The teachings of *tasawwuf* come directly from the Holy Qur'an and the Science of Prophethood, which uses the practices the Holy Prophet Muhammad ﷺ implemented upon himself. The aim of these practices is to control the ego self (*nafs*), which is a collection of little "i's" such as "i" the dutiful husband, "i" the successful businessman, "i" the good mate, etc.

Most people identify their real selves with their ego selves and this is a mistake. When we are born our real self is present but there is no ego self or personality. The ego self (*nafs*) is the mask we construct in response to the things that happen to us during our lives. In order to rediscover our real selves and become closer to Allah, we must totally bring our *nafs* under control and harmonise the little "i's," spiritualising them and thus transforming them in such a way that the Real "I," the Higher Self or Divine Within, can be known and expressed in everyday life.

The Sufis do this by following the Sacred Law of Islam (*shari'ah*). The *shari'ah* provides the Sufi with a framework for living within a community. It sets out everything, when he should fast, how much charity he should give, how he should deal with his fellow men, how often he should pray, what he should eat, how he should eat, how to perform ablutions, how to pray, the laws of marriage and inheritance – according to the wishes of the Divine, not those of man.

The *shari'ah* is a method for taming the *nafs* and disciplining its negative aspects. The Sufi not only lives in accordance with these laws but also tries to go further. He attempts to follow the practices that the Holy Prophet Muhammad ﷺ implemented upon himself (*sunnah*). He does this to increase his awareness and expand his consciousness. The Holy Prophet ﷺ is known as the Universal Man (*al-insan al-kamil*); he is the ideal to which all Sufis aspire.

The Heart

The Holy Prophet Muhammad ﷺ said, "Truly in the body there is a morsel of flesh which, if it be whole, all the body is whole and which, if it be diseased, all of it is diseased. Truly, it is the heart" (*Sahih Muslim*).

And he ﷺ also said, "The hearts rust just as the iron does. There is a polish for everything to remove rust and the polish for the heart is the Remembrance of Allah (*dhikrullah*)" (*Musnad Shahab*).

Tasawwuf, which derives from the Arabic word *safa*, to purify, is the method of polishing, cleansing, and purifying the heart. To cleanse the heart of everything that is "other than Allah," so that Allah may take up His residence there. The method used is the Remembrance of Allah (*dhikrullah*). The ultimate remembrance is that which is perpetual and silent, with one's heart. When the heart has been polished, through the *dhikr*, it then awakens into constant awareness of its Lord.

"My eyes may sleep, but my heart remains awake," said the Holy Prophet Muhammad ﷺ (*Sahih Muslim*).

This perpetual *dhikr*, or constant awareness, is alluded to in another *hadith*, "He whose being does not vibrate at the Remembrance of the Friend has no friend."

The Friend is Allah, and the vibrations which are activated by the *dhikrullah*, are the never-ending agitation of every atom within the body of the one who remembers.

Balance, harmony, peace, and tranquillity can all be attained through the Remembrance of Allah - perfect balance of one's inner and outer existence, harmony with all of the creation, and peace and tranquillity of the self. Before there can be peace, however, there must be a conflict, a great battle, which will subdue the internal enemies and bring them under control.

Once, when they were returning from a battle, the Holy Prophet Muhammad ﷺ said to some of his companions, "We have returned from the Lesser Holy War to the Greater Holy War" (*Kanz al-Ummal*). When one of them asked: "What is the Greater Holy War, Oh Messenger of Allah?" He answered, "The war against the self."

And he ﷺ also said, "The worst enemy you have is (the self) between your sides" (*Sunan Bayhaqi*).

Spiritual Psychology

The warfare takes place between three "centres of energy," the *nafs* (the lower self), the *qalb* (the heart or intelligent self), and the *ruh* (the spiritual or intuitive self).

The *nafs* is the force that binds us to our physical existence. Its pull is downwards towards the fulfilment of sensual desires and bodily needs, towards fame and flattery. The *nafs* is like an untamed horse. If the rider does not master it, leaving it to run wild and do as it pleases, it will cause upheaval and destruction. But if the animal is tamed and carefully disciplined to follow its master's command, it becomes the vehicle by which he arrives at his true destination – the Abode of Peace. The untamed *nafs* is often spoken of in the Holy Qur'an:

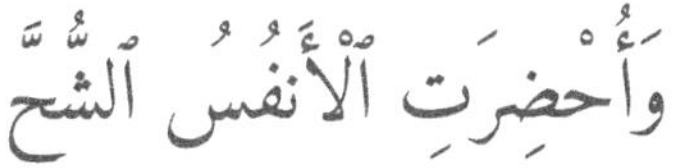

The selves of men have been made prone to greed

(Holy Qur'an 4:128)

إِنَّ ٱلنَّفْسَ لَأَمَّارَةٌ بِٱلسُّوءِ

The (human) soul is certainly prone to evil
(Holy Qur'an 12:53)

This incitement to evil has to be curbed by the intelligent and the intuitional parts of the self, the *qalb* (the heart) and the *ruh* (spirit).

The *ruh* is exactly the opposite of the *nafs*. Whereas the *nafs*, the selfish self, is always pulling man earthwards, the *ruh*, the spiritual self, is continually striving to lift him to the heavens. It is the characteristic of the *ruh* that, being near to Allah, it is always reaching out for even more closeness and even more intimacy with Him.

The Holy Qur'an says of man:

فَإِذَا سَوَّيْتُهُ وَنَفَخْتُ فِيهِ مِن رُّوحِي

I have made him and breathed into him of My Spirit
(Holy Qur'an 15:29)

This intense love the *ruh* has for Allah is of its very essence and it has three aspects. One is the sense of utter dependence upon Him, which gives rise to extreme humility and resignation to His Will. The second is the desire to please Him, to spend oneself for His purposes and to sacrifice all for Him. The third, the highest aspiration of the *ruh*, is to achieve union with Him, to become the mirror of His Light and to abandon his own imperfection by becoming the reflection of His Perfection. The *ruh* is also turned towards his fellow spirits, those of other men. The *ruh* gives to other souls and also absorbs strength and light from them – they contribute to each other's development and flowering.

The *ruh*, the spiritual self, continually sheds its light on the *qalb*, the intelligent self (or the heart), trying to exercise his upward attraction on it. This is the battlefield.

The *qalb* is placed between the two opposite forces, the *nafs* and the *ruh*. They attract him, now upwards, now downwards, and it is he who has to weigh and assess their promptings, to discriminate between them, to decide and then enforce his decision through the will. The *qalb* is the seat of human responsibility. Stationed between the selfish and the spiritual selves, the *qalb* is the arbitrator and the moderator of their conflicts and the harmoniser of their discords. Equilibrium is the giving to everything its due, the weighing of opposites in the balance and delivering the correct decision. The whole drama of human answerability for actions is enacted here.

Initially the influence of the *nafs* is strong and immediate, and that of the *ruh* is weak and distant. Its rays sometimes play upon the *qalb*, producing only a vague and little understood longing for the Sublime and the Ultimate. The *qalb* does not grasp the meaning. It is only when the fundamentals of existence are revealed to him by Allah, through His Illuminating Message, that he comes to know of his origin. The *qalb* hears the words and the *ruh* thrills to the music of Truth and speaks to the ear of the *qalb*, saying, "Accept it, it is true, it is true!"

Then, if the *qalb* accepts the light of faith, if the potentiality becomes an actuality, he becomes firmly set on his way to

Allah. The *qalb* and the *ruh* interact upon each other and go forward to their destination.

If, however, the *qalb* does not accept the Message, and is so darkened by the influence of the *nafs* by completely denying the spiritual, it becomes one of the "rejectors" who, by turning away from Truth, put themselves on the path to ruin.

When the Holy Prophet Muhammad ﷺ was asked how his *shaytaan* (lower qualities) behaved, he answered, "*Aslama shaytaani* (my lower self has become a Muslim) and does whatever I order him" (*Sahih Muslim*). All the lower faculties and instincts had been turned into useful tools in the service of Allah.

The Spiritual Master

Just as for every branch of knowledge and science a tutor is necessary, so in the science of soul purification a pure Master is required.

"He who has no *Shaykh, Shaytaan* will be his guide," said the Holy Prophet Muhammad ﷺ.

Making an attempt to progress on the Spiritual Path without a Guide is mere vanity. If such a person starts to progress in the worship of Allah, arrogance and self-conceit begin to grow in him and he comes to think that he is one of the good believers. This is a great mistake, for the welfare of a person's Islam rests upon his believing that he is a thing of no value, a non-entity. When one sits with an attitude of respect before his Spiritual Master (a *Murshid* or *Shaykh*), arrogance leaves his heart because he acknowledges the fact that he knows nothing of himself and has come to his Master to learn, to be transformed, to journey to his Higher Self.

The word "master" implies the existence of a "slave." To become the sincere disciple (*murid*) of a Spiritual Master (*Murshid*) one must be prepared to totally hand over his will to the Master and be as a slave in carrying out all of the Master's requests.

The Spiritual Master appears to be living in the physical arena, but, in reality, he is centred in the world of the spirit. He is directly connected to the Source of the Sufi Teaching. He has made the Journey back to his own root, which is the state of non-existence in the Knowledge of Allah. Only he is able to take the hand of his disciple (*murid*) and guide him through the many dangerous and frightening valleys of the self as they journey together, from the lower self to the Higher Self.

The qualified *Shaykh* or *Murshid* possesses as a gift of Allah, the power of transference of spiritual qualities as a kind of outpouring from the always full vessel of his heart. By means of this power he is continually aiding the *murid* in the development of his inner potentialities, correcting his aberrations and supporting his efforts in the proper direction.

Bay'ah

Bay'ah is the Pact of Initiation that a *murid* takes at the hand of his or her Spiritual Master on the occasion of entering upon the Spiritual Path (*tariqa*). *Bay'ah* is a contract for life and continues into the hereafter. Whoever makes this pledge should make it with this awareness. It is a pact not only with the Spiritual Master (*Murshid*), but with all of the saints of the *silsilat* (chain), and, through them, with the Prophet Muhammad ﷺ and, ultimately, with Allah Himself.

إِنَّ ٱلَّذِينَ يُبَايِعُونَكَ إِنَّمَا يُبَايِعُونَ ٱللَّهَ يَدُ ٱللَّهِ فَوْقَ أَيْدِيهِمْ

Verily they who pledge unto thee their allegiance pledge it unto none but Allah. The Hand of Allah is above their hands
(Holy Qur'an 48:10)

The Method of *Tasawwuf*

Life is a journey. From Allah we come and to Allah we return. The purpose of life is to develop spiritually so that we return consciously and to do this a method is needed.

The science of *tasawwuf* is the safest method because the teaching is passed on to the seeker by one who already has what the seeker is looking for. Even with the *shari'ah* to guide him and assist in his self-discipline, he will not be able to completely subdue the *nafs* on his own; although, by the Grace of Allah, he may achieve a certain level of success. A genuine teacher is required to guide the seeker along the path.

The Sufi teacher must be one who has already discovered how to draw near to Allah using the methods of the Holy Qur'an and the teachings of the Holy Prophet ﷺ, which are the sources from which the Sufi method comes. The Sufi teacher has already travelled the path and knows the way and so is able to guide others, warn them of the dangers, and alert them to the subtle tricks of the *nafs*. He will also be connected to one or more Sufi schools and so will be able to confer *baraka* (spiritual blessings), safety, and protection upon the traveller. He will instruct the aspirant in a spiritual program that is specific to his needs and may include such practices as *dhikr* (remembrance of Allah), *dhikr* with specific breathing techniques, fasts, and Qur'anic readings. All of the practices of *tasawwuf* are aimed at the same thing – remembrance of Allah.

Ultimately, the remembrance of Allah with every heartbeat and every breath.

The Practices of *Tasawwuf*

The practices of *tasawwuf* are many and they are chosen to suit a particular individual's needs.

Adab

Adab is defined as ethics or etiquette. It is the proper way of conduct or "manners" of the *murid* (seeker). Some Sufi Masters have said that *Tasawwuf* **is** *adab*. The higher one is in their manner of behaviour, thought, and speech, the higher they are in their development of consciousness. The currency of the Path is virtues.

Dhikr

The most common practice is *dhikr* (sometimes written as *zikr*). This is pronounced so that the "dh" sounds like the "th" in that. *Dhikr* is remembrance of Allah and involves the repetition of certain formulas or Names of

Allah. The particular formula or Name, and the number of repetitions, will be different for each individual. *Dhikr* may be performed individually or in a group setting, known as a *halqah* (circle). Remembrance of Allah can be performed silently or aloud. *Dhikrullah* is a most powerful practice that is able to transform the disciple's consciousness and incinerate his accumulated bad qualities because the Names used in the remembrance are the Names the Divine gave to Himself.

In a Holy Saying (*hadith qudsi*) through the Prophet Muhammad ﷺ, Allah says, "I am with the one who remembers Me" (*Sahih Bukhari*).

The one on the Sufi Path is striving to have Allah with him constantly. The whole art or science of *tasawwuf* consists in perfecting the *dhikr* and in making it perpetual, so that even in the midst of activity it continues to sing in the heart. The heart that has been emptied of all debris, through purification, discipline, and by means of the *dhikr*, is fit to become the dwelling place of Allah Almighty.

"The Heavens and the Earth do not contain Me, but the heart of my believing slave contains Me" (*hadith qudsi*).

Dhikr is the sword which will cut down the enemy in the Greater Holy War against the lower self and its base tendencies.

Dhikr acts directly upon the heart, strengthening it and purifying it, in readiness to become the fit dwelling place for its Lord.

Dhikr is the key to the heart.

Anyone can perform *dhikr*, but perpetual *dhikr* can only be attained at the hand of the Spiritual Master.

وَأْتُوا ٱلْبُيُوتَ مِنْ أَبْوَٰبِهَا

Enter the houses by their doors

(Qur'an 2:189)

The door to Knowledge of Allah has been set up by Allah and by the Holy Prophet Muhammad ﷺ. Only the inheritors of the Holy Prophet ﷺ are qualified to open those doors for others.

Who are the inheritors of the Holy Prophet ﷺ? They are the Sufi *Shaykhs*, who, through the *silsilats* (chains of transmission), are connected directly to the Holy Prophet ﷺ himself. Any attempt to enter this house by other than its door is not only futile, but also displays the utmost discourtesy towards Allah and His Prophet ﷺ.

Fasting

In addition to fasting the month of *Ramadhan* like all Muslims, the Sufi undertakes voluntary fasts to help subdue the *nafs*. This fasting is different to what is normally considered as fasting in the West. An Islamic fast consists of eating a small meal called *suhoor* about an hour and a half before sunrise, then neither eating nor drinking until just after the sun sets, when the fast is broken with a few dates and some water, then a meal following. Sexual relations and smoking are also prohibited during the hours of fasting.

The traveller on the Path is concerned with fasting on a higher level than that of the body alone. During the time of the fast, he will do his best to abstain from wrong thoughts, speech, and actions as well. Most voluntary fasts take place on Monday, Thursday, and the 13-15th days of the lunar month. In addition to these, the Sufi teacher may direct the disciple to undertake other supervised fasts as well.

Prayer

In addition to the five daily prayers (*salat*), the Sufi may offer extra, voluntary prayers. These may be *sunnah* prayers, which are extra prayers the Holy Prophet ﷺ used to pray before and after the compulsory prayers, or they may be extra prayers performed at times specified by the Sufi teacher.

One particular prayer favoured by the Sufis is called *tahajjud* and is performed at some time between '*isha* (the night prayer) and *fajr* (the morning prayer). *Tahajjud* prayers consist of two cycles (*rakats*) of prayer that are prolonged by reciting certain passages of the Holy Qur'an. This practice was recommended to the Holy Prophet Muhammad ﷺ in the Holy Qur'an and he recommended it to his followers.

Seclusion

In this teaching as in every teaching, we need to set aside a few days specifically to concentrate on the spiritual work that has been given and for which, in everyday life, there is no opportunity. Seclusion (*khalwa*) is always done under the strict supervision of the Sufi Teacher. The period of seclusion may be for as little as one day or for as long as 40 days. During this time the *murid* will be given special *dhikr* to perform and his food intake will be gradually reduced as he becomes less focused on the body and more focused on the inner work.

Qur'an readings

The Teacher may direct the *murid* to read particular sections of the Qur'an for particular purposes and in a particular manner or he may direct the disciple to contemplate and reflect on one passage. This is in addition to whatever the disciple wishes to read from the Qur'an on a daily basis.

Muhasabah

Muhasabah is the act of taking account. Each day the seeker should look back over his actions and thoughts. He should repent of any misconduct or bad thoughts and make the intention not to repeat them. The Sufi follows the directive "take account of your self before an account is taken from you."

Muraqabah

Muraqabah refers to "vigilant concentration" or meditation and visualisation. During the *dhikr*, the *murid* will concentrate on visualising the Name of Allah as shown below. This will keep him focused and enable him to resist unwanted thoughts and bring about a state of *hudur* (being totally present).

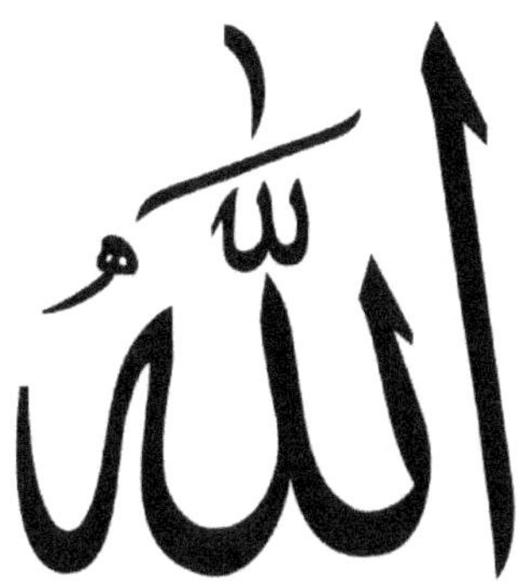

Dreams

The physical and the spiritual are different in degree, not in kind. If we use the analogy of water, we would say the physical body is like ice and the spiritual body like steam. We live our "waking state" in this realm with the physical body and, when we become in touch with the Real within ourselves, it comes to us in our dreams. Dreams are a very important and sacred part of the teaching as they indicate the state of consciousness of the disciple. It is very important to keep the dreams private and only share them with the Sufi Teacher to whom he can take them for interpretation.

Sufi Dancing

This is not really dancing in the generally accepted sense of the word. By the term "Sufi dancing," most people are referring to the whirling performed by the dervishes of the Mevlevi Order of Sufis founded by Shaykh Jalaluddin Rumi. Before being given permission to perform the whirling, a dervish must have had many years of spiritual training. The whirling is performed under the guidance of a Sufi Teacher who ensures the safety of the dervishes while they are in a state of ecstasy induced by the practice.

Sufi Poetry

Sufi poetry is often regarded as merely beautiful love poetry. To describe it in this way is to do it a great disservice. Sufi poetry was written by the great masters and saints of *tasawwuf* such as Shaykh Rumi, Jami, Yunus

Emre, Rabia al-Adawiyyah, and Omar Khayyam and is used to express the intense love felt for the Beloved Allah. It often contains spiritual instruction by way of teaching stories, as in Rumi's *Mathnawi*, and can contain highly mystical knowledge concealed as verse.

To truly appreciate such poetry, one needs to read translations by people who are themselves travellers upon the Path. Otherwise, major inferences may be lost by those who do not understand.

Sufi Stories

Sufi stories are, without exception, teaching stories, although their purpose is not always self-evident. The great Master Idries Shah has made a vast number of these stories available to people in the western world. The most famous of these stories are perhaps the ones concerning the antics of Mulla Nasrudin.

Sufi stories work on many levels: emotional, intellectual, and spiritual. They often release their meaning slowly over a period of time so that on first reading one gains certain information and then, perhaps a year or so later, one understands a different aspect of the tale.

The Journey

The aim of the spiritual work that is given to the disciple is to assist him to traverse the seven stages of the self, from the *nafs al-ammarratan bi su'* (the Animal Self) through to the *nafs al-kamila* (the Perfect Self). The names given to the different stages of the self are specifically mentioned in the Holy Qur'an.

Each stage of the journey of the Self has its own particular characteristics and these are shown below:

1. *Nafs al-Ammarratan bi su'* (The Animal Self)

This is the lower self. It is very strong and has many clever tricks to turn us away from the journey. However, like a good horse, once it is trained it will provide us with transport for the journey. The world of the Animal Self is the world of the senses. All sensual and material pleasures are connected to the Animal Self. The main condition of the self at this level is desire. Qualities associated with the Animal Self are miserliness, stinginess, arrogance, love of fame, envy, heedlessness, and forgetfulness.

In order to continue on the journey, the self needs discipline. We must no longer do things automatically; we need to be aware of every action and every thought and we need to cultivate acceptance which is the antidote to desire. Accept each moment and what it contains rather than desiring something else.

2. *Nafs al-Lawwama* (The Complaining Self)

The Complaining Self represents the development of conscience. This is the intermediate world between animal and angelic. The condition of the Self at this stage is that of love and the qualities it exhibits are: complaining, thinking, contraction, perplexity, questioning, and rejecting.

This is really the awakening of the Self to things other than the material, the development of love, and the seeking of a higher reality. To develop the Self further, one needs a guide, a Sufi Teacher or *Murshid*, who has travelled the road and knows its pitfalls and wrong turns. The *Murshid* should be connected to a genuine Sufi school. This ensures the correctness of the teaching and also confers protection and spiritual blessing upon the seeker.

3. *Nafs al-Mulhamma* (The Inspired Self)

The world of the Inspired Self is the angelic world and the condition of the Self at this stage is that of Divine Passion. Qualities associated with this stage are: generosity, satisfaction, knowledge, humility, repentance, patience, and doing good to others while accepting the bad they may do to us.

Development from this point takes place through gnosis, which is why it is called the stage of the Inspired Self.

4. *Nafs al-Mutma'inna* (The Self at Peace)

The world of the Self at Peace is the Reality of the Universal Man. The condition of the Self at this point is reunion and the qualities expressed are: a higher state of generosity, trusting in God, worship, gratitude, and acceptance.

The method used by the Self for development at this point is REALITY.

5. *Nafs ar-Radhiyya* (The Well Pleased Self).

The world of the Well Pleased Self is the world of Divinity and its condition is annihilation within the Divinity. Because of this, there is no further method with which to continue the journey. Any further progress is purely by the Grace of the Divine.

Qualities expressed by the Self at this stage are: renunciation, truthfulness, alertness, leaving that which does not concern us in all things, and fulfilling promises.

6. *Nafs al-Mardhiyya* (The Well Pleasing Self)

The world of the *Well Pleasing Self* is witnessing and its condition is bewilderment. The method used to progress from here is once again self-discipline, but obviously this time the awareness would be of a much higher order.

The qualities exhibited by the Well Pleasing Self are: implementing the higher qualities of spiritual etiquette, leaving everything other than God, kindness to all creations, using all our means to get closer to God, contemplating on the greatness of God, and accepting what God has destined for us.

7. *Nafs al-Kamila* (The Perfect Self)

The world of the Perfect Self is multiplicity in unity and unity in multiplicity and hence its condition is one of seeing God established in everything. Although this is the last stage, it is not the end of the journey. Because God is limitless, the path of development is also limitless.

Progress within this last stage encompasses all of the methods that went before. Qualities exhibited by someone who has reached this stage are all of the good qualities mentioned from the earlier stages – and only God knows best.

While a seeker is passing through these stages, he could well be seduced by the attractions of some of them such as clairvoyance, the ability to heal, or other uses of psychic or floating energies. It is because of this that the need for a genuine Sufi Master is so great, otherwise, the seeker may well become so engrossed in a "by product" of development that he forgets his aim and his journey and becomes lost forever. The Sufis say that whoever does not have a genuine guide, *Shaytaan* (the devil) will become his guide. In other words, he will be tempted all of the way and may succumb to these temptations, forgetting that they are not his true goal.

The disciple should not be concerned as to where he is on the journey as the illusion will be very strong. He should keep his attention focused on the aim and know his Teacher is well aware of his progress. The trust between the *Murshid* and the *murid* will take care of his progress. The reason for this is some of the stages of development have certain attractions which, if the *murid* paid attention to them, would strengthen the ego self by puffing it up with pride and he would get stuck. The *Murshid* is always alert in case the disciple veers off course and he gently (or not) steers him back.

The path of the Sufi is unlike that found in most esoteric systems because it does not require withdrawal from the world. In fact, one of the aims of the teaching is to be in the world but not of the world – to live in this world as a stranger passing through.

The Sufis know the truth of the saying, "As is the microcosm, so is the macrocosm." The microcosm is man, each man, and the macrocosm is the universe. If we want to really change the world from the condition it is in, each of us has to change ourself, because what is out there is only a mirror of what is in here!!!

The seven stages of the journey to God are described in *tasawwuf* as follows:

Journeying to Allah

Journeying for Allah

Journeying under the care of Allah

Journeying with Allah

Journeying within Allah

Journeying from Allah

Journeying by Allah

How to Begin the Journey

You don't have to withdraw from the world to practice the teachings of *tasawwuf*. In fact, monasticism is frowned upon in Islam. Our aim is to fulfil the injunction of the Holy Prophet Muhammad ﷺ when he said "Be in this world but not of it" (*Sahih Bukhari*).

Every journey starts with one step, but how do you take the first step to *tasawwuf*? First one has to have the realisation that there is so much that we do not know about Reality. Not until one is prepared to throw away all his preconceptions about the world, life, and God is he a suitable vessel for the teaching.

One thing the seeker must be clear on is that the Sufis **know** Allah, **know** the Truth, **know** the Real. What they teach is not theory, surmise, or philosophy; it is knowledge of the Real.

One can begin the journey by reading books on *tasawwuf* and these days there are many wonderful books by Sufi Masters available in English. One can also begin to humble himself and attempt to empty his heart in order that when the time is right, it may be filled with *himma*, that painful yet sweet longing to know Allah, to become as close to Allah as He is to us. When the seeker has truly emptied himself and knows that he can do nothing by himself then the *tariqa* will find him and his Teacher will become apparent.

بسم الله الرحمن الرحيم

Tasawwuf in Australia

We are fortunate that in the West there are many genuine Sufi Centres available to us and this applies to Australia as well. The Almiraj Sufi and Islamic Study Centre provides the teaching of *tasawwuf* to sincere seekers wishing to once and for all transform themselves into Real Human Beings.

A Brief Outline of the Centre

There are many things in today's world which are designed specifically to distract us and keep us away from finding that which is Real. The aim of the Study Centre is to provide an environment where true seekers of knowledge can come and be filled with the pure, spiritual food of Islam, without superstition, fairytales, or artificial teachings.

The Almiraj Sufi and Islamic Study Centre is connected to the Burhaniyya-Dasuqiyya-Shadhiliyya *tariqa* and the table that is set encompasses all of the teachings of the Holy

Prophet Muhammad ﷺ. There are many books available for study, written by saintly teachers throughout the history of Islam. The most important foundation to build upon is that of the Holy Qur'an, the verified Hadiths, and the science of Prophethood (what the Holy Prophet ﷺ implemented upon himself).

The spiritual director of the Study Centre is Murshid F. A. Ali ElSenossi and it is under his guidance and supervision we travel this Path to Allah.

The Bookshop and Sufi Study Centre have relocated several times before finding a permanent home in Broken Hill.

The Goals of the Centre

❋ To introduce Islam in its totality to the community.

❋ To work with the psychological spiritual teaching of Islam (*tasawwuf*) so that the higher teaching of the Unity of Allah will be explained clearly to all who seek to know Allah through the teaching of Islam.

❋ To find a suitable channel of communication with all other organisations and systems of personal development, and we have found that the development of the Self through the teaching of Islamic Sufism is the best way to introduce Islam.

❋ To hold weekly meetings of the Sufi Study Group.

❋ To give talks to community groups, colleges, and universities to introduce the psychological spiritual teaching of Islam (*tasawwuf*).

To donate books to libraries, colleges, universities, and schools and, through the bookshop, to provide access to literature on all aspects of Islamic teaching. Special emphasis is placed on the study of personal development through works on Islamic Sufism, which have been written by eminent, highly respected Muslims from around the world.

To publish, in English, contemporary accounts of journeys within *tasawwuf* to demonstrate the relevance of this great teaching to the people of today's Western societies.

And, most of all, to build bridges between human beings and the societies they form so that harmony and peace will prevail. Islam – peace – both inward and outward – will be the order of the day.

In Brief

❁ Knowledge of Allah can only be attained by travelling the Sufi Path.

❁ The heart can only become purified for this Knowledge by practising the *dhikrullah*.

❁ The *dhikrullah* can only be truly effective when given to the *murid* by the *Murshid* (Spiritual Master).

❁ One cannot become a *murid* of a *Murshid* except by taking *bay'ah*.

❁ The one who takes *bay'ah* must be prepared to carry out his Master's requests with an attitude of complete devotion and love.

❁ To be devoted to the *Murshid* is to be devoted to the Holy Prophet ﷺ, which is to be devoted to Allah Almighty.

✻ There is only one Light, shining from the Source of all Light – ALLAH, through the Holy Prophet ﷺ, to his inheritors, the Sufi Shaykhs, and into the hearts of their devoted *murids*.

ٱلَّذِينَ ءَامَنُواْ وَتَطْمَئِنُّ قُلُوبُهُم بِذِكْرِ ٱللَّهِ أَلَا بِذِكْرِ ٱللَّهِ تَطْمَئِنُّ ٱلْقُلُوبُ

Those who believe, and whose hearts find satisfaction in the remembrance of Allah: for without doubt in the remembrance of Allah do hearts find satisfaction

(Holy Qur'an 13:28)

Enquiries about Sufi Studies and Sufi Books should be directed to:

Almiraj Sufi and Islamic Study Centre
158 Argent Street
Broken Hill,
NSW, Australia 2880

Phone: +61 8 8088 1019

www.almirajsuficentre.org.au
nasihah@almirajsuficentre.org.au
info@sufibooks.com.au

And the last of our prayer is *Alhamdulillahi Rabbil 'Alamein.*

Recommended Reading

The Holy Qur'an, translation by Abdullah Yusuf Ali

Sahih Bukhari

Muhammad: His Life Based on the Earliest Sources, Martin Lings

Fat-Hud Dayyan Fi Fighi Khairil Adyan: Opening towards understanding the Best of Religions, Muhammad Ibn Ahmad Lebbai

Islam: Beliefs and Teachings, Ghulam Sarwar

The Language of the Future: Book of Sufi Terminology, Murshid F.A. Ali ElSenossi

Kashf al-Mahjub: Unveiling the Veiled, Syed Ali bin Uthman al-Hujweri

Sufi Book of Spiritual Ascent: al-Risala al-Qushayriyya, Abu'l-Qasim al-Qushayri

The Book of Sufi Healing, Shaykh Chishti

Realities of Sufism, Shaykh 'Abd al-Qadir 'Isa

Irshad: *Wisdom of a Sufi Master*, Sheikh Muzaffer Ozak al-Jerrahi

Sufism - A Beginners Guide, William Chittick

The Sufi Path of Knowledge, William Chittick

What is Sufism?, Martin Lings

An Introduction to Sufism, Titus Burckhardt

The Vision of Islam, Sachiko Murata and William Chittick

Glossary

adab: spiritual courtesy, etiquette, manners. It is spiritual courtesy and gracious behaviour of the Path and perfect refinement of words and deeds. *Adab* is giving each thing and each moment its proper due. The science of the higher teaching is based upon *adab*, which encompasses all human life. It extends from right behaviour with regard to the Sacred Law (*shari'ah*), right behaviour with one's fellow travellers, proper conduct towards the teaching and one's teacher, and reaches to unceasing spiritual courtesy to Allah Himself. The proper courtesy towards the Law is to stay within its boundaries. The proper conduct with regards to good actions is to complete the action and disconnect from it. *Adab* with regard to the Real is knowing what belongs to oneself and what belongs to Allah. Each moment and each situation have its own *adab*. It has been said that the higher teaching is all *adab* and the greater your understanding and implementation of proper conduct is, the higher you are in the teaching.

baraka: Spiritual energy. It is a subtle spiritual energy which flows through everything, though strongest within the human. The more purified the human becomes, the greater the flow of *baraka*. Overpowering *baraka* can be experienced in sacred places, in sacred art, and in sanctified people, all of which are theophanies, revealing and manifesting the Divinity – here on earth.

batin: Inward knowledge. The science of inward knowledge as opposed to the "exterior" science (*'ilm al-thahir*) of the Doctors of Law. The knower possesses both the inward and outward knowledges because he "knows" Allah and Allah is both the Nonmanifest (*al-batin*) and the Manifest (*al-thahir*). Knowledge of Allah necessarily encompasses both the Inward and the Outward aspects of existence.

bay'ah: Pledge of Initiation. The pledge or rite of initiation into a Sufi *tariqa*. This pledge, which in truth is a pledge between Allah and His slave, eternally bonds together the Murshid and his *murid*. Within the *bay'ah* there is a sacred moment in which the spiritual energy of the spiritual chain is transmitted from the Murshid to the *murid*. This enables the *murid* to travel in safety under Divine Protection and with Divine Aid.

deen: Life Transaction. The word *deen* indicates the life transaction between Allah and Man. It is not merely religion in the constricted and limited sense, which the word has assumed in these times. This life transaction is between Allah and man, between the Creator and the created, the Limitless and the limited, the One and the many. Life transaction includes every facet, every aspect of life – from the smallest detail to the greatest action. Every moment of a man's life should be impregnated with the awareness of Allah – life is meaningless and futile without such an awareness. Islam, the Perfect and Final Revelation, is the Straight Path to this awareness of the Source. The higher teaching is the Living Heart of Islam – the Heart from which flows the life-giving nourishment to every soul in the manifested world.

dhikr: Remembrance. Remembrance, invocation, or glorification of Allah, through the repetition of one of His Names or a phrase to His Glory. True *dhikr* is a Spiritual state in which the one who remembers (*dhakir*) concentrates all his physical and spiritual powers upon Allah so that his entire being may be united with the Absolute. It is the fundamental practice of the Sufi path and may be undertaken in solitude or in gatherings. Specific breathing patterns are central to the effectiveness of the *dhikr*.

dhikrullah: Remembrance of Allah. Invocation of Allah through one of His Names or through His Words. The perfect *dhikrullah*, in which Allah becomes the seeing, the hearing, the speaking, the grasping of the one who remembers, is attained when every atom of the *dhakir*'s being is absorbed and annihilated in the Remembrance of Allah. The *dhakir* becomes internally unified with the Absolute. Only then does Allah sit totally with the one who remembers Allah.

hadith (pl. *ahadith*): Saying of the Holy Prophet Muhammad ﷺ.

hadith qudsi: Holy saying. These are the Sacred Words of Allah Almighty speaking through the Holy Prophet Muhammad ﷺ. They are a separate type of Revelation to that of the Qur'an. The sayings (Holy sayings and Prophetic sayings) form one of the foundations of the higher teaching.

hajj: Pilgrimage to the Sacred Mosque, the House of Allah, at the Centre of Mecca. *Hajj* is the ultimate journey to the knowledge of Allah Who dwells in the secret centre of the human heart. Here the treasury of spiritual realities is to be discovered. The pilgrim travels to the Sacred Centre mounted on his spiritual resolve, his overwhelming love, and his yearning for the Beloved. Mecca is the place of the House of Allah, where the slave stands alone before his Lord. Mecca is total inwardness and bewilderment. Mecca is Reality. After performing the *hajj* go to the grave of the Chosen One (*Mustafa*). After realising the Unity of Allah, after being annihilated in Oneness, return to the Muhammadan Presence, because, once you know Allah, then you will know who *Rasulullah* is! Visit Holy Mecca and then visit Holy Medina. The Islamic pilgrimage is one of the ethics of the Sufis. It is the goal they try to achieve. The pilgrimage of the Sufi is in a whole other category from that of the ordinary Muslim. As far as the pilgrimage to Mecca in Saudi Arabia, most perform it once in a lifetime, following the method of the Holy Prophet Muhammad ﷺ. Of those who perform the pilgrimage numerous times, many choose to live in the neighbourhood of Mecca and maintain the highest *adab* and spiritual practices to remain there. The real pilgrimage in Sufi terminology is the continuation of seeking nearness to Allah.

hijra: Migration. *Hijra* is to leave one's homeland in the Way of Allah (*fi sabilillah*). For the lovers of Allah, this migration is from the corporeal world to the world of the spirits. It is a departure from one's sins and errors and the abandonment of one's will.

himma: Intense spiritual resolve. This is the most powerful force contained within man. It is the sincere and dedicated application of all of one's efforts and strivings towards attaining the desired Object - Allah. The strength of this will results from its sincerity and the purity of its facing, its collectedness, and its focusing on a specific matter. *Himma* is a pure, active force in the human being and is found in the origin of his creation and nature, or else it is acquired and developed later. From the point of view of it being a force, it is capable of attachment and is therefore attached in accordance with the will of its owner. If one attaches one's *himma* to the world, one achieves riches and position; if one attaches it to worship, one achieves stations and inspirations; and if it belongs to Allah, all attachments fallaway and the aspiration becomes one. *Himma* is to turn totally to the Creative Truth without saying "I can't" or, with regards to the self, "what's in it for me?" By using the means and the connections of work and the convictions of hope and to trust yourself with it totally. In the beginning, *himma* is that you have made firm your convictions towards obedience to Allah and fulfilling the promise of your repentance. It can develop from there and it is possible for the spiritual resolve to proceed through the following stages: The connection of one's heart by the real blessing that never diminishes. Swaying the self from the diminishing desires. Seriousness in seeking the Truth when there is reluctance. With regards to conduct, *himma* is 1. The desire to remain steadfast in the spiritual actions one performs. 2. With the continuation of visualisation and the power of trust in Allah, by doing what you need to do, and you surrender to Him. With regards to manners, one should turn the *himma* totally towards proper behaviour in order to achieve the ultimate happiness and completeness. With regards to foundations, the *himma* will pull her owner towards the right of the Creative Truth by the power of the Grace of Allah. And the peace and tranquillity of being with Allah will not stop her owner or cool down. Through their spiritual resolve the great friends of Allah possess the power to perform miracles. Yet, due to their knowledge, their slavehood, and their perfect courtesy they refrain from exercising such spiritual resolve except when in compliance with a Divine Command. There can be no greater blessing for a human than the gift of being born into this earthly realm with the pre-eternal yearning to return to his Origin. It is the greatest gift that Allah gives to anyone. And, it is the highest luck, because this yearning, this *himma*, was established within the as yet unformed soul when it was still non-existent, though existent within the Knowledge of

Allah. The opposites become united in such a human, who, though dwelling in an earthly body of clay and decomposition, has a yearning soul, composed of the noble virtues and immortal qualities. For this Gift, the seeker will never be able to express his thanks to his Lord. He who has no spiritual aspiration or sincere will in seeking Allah in gratitude or in love cannot have an ambition to follow the Sufi Path of Friendship.

hudur: Presence with Allah. *Hudur* is the heart's presence with Allah when it is absent from everything else. The slave can never be present with Allah except through one of His Beautiful Names and in so doing a state of perfect spiritual courtesy is maintained.

al-insan al-kamil: Perfect Man. He is the viceregent of Allah, through whom Allah contemplates His Own Name derived Perfection. The Perfect Man has actualized the divine form and, in carrying the Trust, has fulfilled his reason for being. It is through the Perfect Man that Allah enters the world. *al-Insan al-Kamil* is also one of the names given to the Supreme Isthmus. Man consists of a body and a spirit which governs it. The cosmos also consists of a body and a spirit which governs it. Its spirit is the Perfect Man. Without him the cosmos is likened to a discarded body.

islam: Surrender. The Journey of Return to Allah is from the first *islam* which is merely verbal submission, through the levels of ascent to the second and real *islam*, which is total and unconditional surrender with knowledge and love to the Will of Allah. The seven levels of knowledge through which the traveller (*salik*) must pass are Surrender, Belief, Perfection, Knowledge of Certainty, Eye of Certainty, Truth of Certainty, and unconditional surrender with Knowledge. Islam means peace and the person who follows this peace is called the Muslim. From another root meaning of the word, Islam means complete submission and surrender, and the person who submits and surrenders himself to the will of his Lord is the person who has accepted Allah as his Creator, Sustainer, Lord, and the Master of the Day of Judgement. So, from both the definitions Islam means a way of life for people who have opted to follow peace as opposed to chaos, order as opposed to disorder, discipline as opposed to indiscipline, submission as opposed to refusal, surrender as opposed to insolence, obedience as opposed to disobedience etc. All these things combined define Islam as a way of life by which a person becomes a follower of peace and not a follower of chaos. And the followers of peace are the Muslims whose duty it is "to establish peace and what is good, and to prevent chaos and what is evil, and they are the best people" (Holy Qur'an 3:110).

jihad al-akbar: Greater Holy War. This is the constant and vigilant inner warfare against ignorance, the passions, and the vices of the lower self which drag man downwards away from Allah. It is the real struggle against the inner enemies, the inner unbelievers and the inner tyrants. The celestial weapon used in the Greater Holy War is the Remembrance of Allah.

ka'aba: The Sacred Centre in Mecca towards which Muslims face for the ritual prayer, bowing and prostrating before Allah. The *ka'aba* is the earthly symbol of the Divine Throne (*al-'arsh*), around which the angels circle and it is a symbol of the sanctified heart of the Perfect Man. The Essence itself (*dhat*).

khawla: The spiritual retreat and seclusion. Initially spiritual retreat is undertaken by physically withdrawing from those outside disturbances which have the potential of distracting one in his contemplation of Allah's Names and Attributes. Ultimately this withdrawal becomes purely spiritual when the heart is in a state of perpetual presence with Allah. Then the lover of Allah is with his Beloved at all times, regardless of the external conditions within which he is situated. *Khalwa* is the conversation of one's secret awareness with Allah.

muhasabah: Taking account. The constant analysis of the heart and its changing states. During *muhasabah* the contemplative takes stock of the heart's most secret motions. He calls himself to account, here and now. He does not wait till the Hereafter.

muraqabah: Concentration, concentrated, meditation. This term applies to the vigilant concentration, with all the power of mind, thought, imagination, and examination through which the slave carefully keeps guard over himself. During his *muraqabah* the slave observes how Allah becomes manifest both in the cosmos and within himself.

murid: Seeker. The one who desires Allah. The *murid* is the seeker of Reality who is under the direction of a Spiritual Guide (*murshid*). He has entered the company of those who concentrate upon Allah through the remembrance of His Most Holy Name "Allah."

murshid: Spiritual Guide. The *murshid* is a true inheritor of the Holy Prophet Muhammad ﷺ. After having been taken to the Divine Presence during his ascension the slave has been returned, by Allah, to the creation to guide and perfect the still imperfect ones. He was taken up as a slave and returned as a slave and *murshid*. The qualities of an authentic *murshid* are those of his own Master and Teacher, the Holy Prophet ﷺ himself. The sacred connection between a *murshid* and his *murids* was established in pre-eternity and continues into eternity. Because of the *murshid's* own spiritual attainments, his *murids* have the possibility of becoming travellers. The perfect *murshid* is of the people of blame and his *murids* sometimes also attain perfection. For the *murid*, the *murshid* is one of the "signs on the horizons," the outward of his own inward. What he sees in the mirror of his *murshid* is a reflection of what is within his own self. He may also see within the *murshid* the good qualities and excellent character traits which are yet latent in himself.

nafs: Self. The ego or the self or the soul. The *nafs* is that dimension of man which stands between the spirit which is light, and the physical body which is darkness. The spiritual struggle or combat is waged against the downward pulling tendencies of the *nafs* which seduce the heart away from Allah. The *nafs* is also the domain of imagination. Allah is within our own selves, yet we do not see Allah. The work of the higher teaching is directed towards transforming the lower self into the higher perfect self and "seeing" Allah everywhere. There are seven stages of the self, seven postures in the ritual prayer, seven verses or "signs" in the opening chapter of the Qur'an, and seven levels of knowledge, all of which are finely interconnected.

Shaykh Mahmoud Taha of Sudan writes concerning the self: "This soul is immortal in essence despite the changes that befall it through different forms and at different times and places. At no time does the soul cease its quest for immortality - to be immortal in form as it is in essence. This story is ... the story of every human being. However, we all have forgotten it. By 'forgetting' it is meant that it settled at the bottom of the unconscious and was then covered by a thick layer of illusions and fears that we inherited from the times of ignorance and superstition. There is no way that we can achieve our happiness unless we break through this thick layer ... which prevents the forms of the unconscious to be reflected in the mirror of the conscious and hence reveal the greater truth, the truth of truths that is shrouded by the veils of light. This long story that flows from the unconscious is made of the same stuff as that of dreams. The Qur'an is made of the same stuff. It was brought into existence only to remind us of our extraordinary story. He who remembers it will acquire knowledge beyond which there is no ignorance and an immortality beyond which there is no perishing."

nafs al-ammarratan bi su': Commanding self. The Qur'an refers to this self, "the (human) soul is certainly prone to evil" (Holy Qur'an 12:53). This self resides in the world of the senses and is dominated by earthly desires and passions. The initial struggle in the early stages of the Spiritual Journey is against the Commanding Self. *Nafs al-ammarratan bi su'* is equated with the first *islam* and the first standing posture of the ritual prayer. The Commanding self is journeying to Allah.

nafs al-kamila: Perfect self. The Qur'an refers to this self, "Enter then, among My slaves. Enter into My Garden" (Holy Qur'an 89:29-30). This is the final stage in the development of the self to the Self. It is the stage of Real Islam when the slave is in a state of perpetual journeying by Allah. The perfect self is equated with the final sitting of the ritual prayer. Attainment of the perfect self is through the Grace of Allah.

nafs al-lawwama: Blaming self. The Qur'an refers to this self, "And I do call to witness the self that blames" (Holy Qur'an 75:2). This self is conscious of its own imperfections. Its journeying is for Allah. The blaming self is equated with the second rung (faith) on the ladder to Knowledge and to the bowing in the ritual prayer. The *nafs al-lawwama* has been set over the greatest of the Sufis, the People of Blame, in order to guard them from any self-conceit.

nafs al-mardhiyya: Well pleasing self. The Qur'an refers to this self, "And well pleasing unto Him!" (Holy Qur'an 89:28). This self is well pleasing to Allah. It experiences the bewilderment of journeying from Allah. The well pleasing self is equated with the sixth rung (truth of certainty) on the ladder to Knowledge and to the second prostration of the ritual prayer.

nafs al-mulhamma: Inspired self. The Qur'an refers to this self, "By the Self and the proportion and order given to it" (Holy Qur'an 91:7). This self has turned away from wrong action and is able to discern that which will take it to felicity. It journeys under the care of Allah. The *nafs al-mulhamma* is equated with the third rung on the ladder to Knowledge (perfection) and to the second standing posture of the ritual prayer.

nafs al-mutma'inna: Peaceful self, the self at peace. The Qur'an refers to this self, "Oh self, in complete rest and satisfaction!" (Holy Qur'an 89:27). This self is tranquil as it rests in the Certitude of Allah. It has been reintegrated into the Spirit. The *nafs al-mutma'inna* journeys with Allah. It is equated with the first prostration of the ritual prayer and with the fourth rung (Knowledge of Certainty) on the ladder to Knowledge.

nafs ar-radhiyya: Well pleased self. The Qur'an refers to this self, "Return to your Lord - well pleased ..." (Holy Qur'an 89:28). This self is well pleased with itself due to the harmonious balance of its noble character traits. It is annihilated in Allah and journeys within Allah. The *nafs ar-radhiyya* is equated with the fifth rung (Eye of Certatinty) on the ladder to Knowledge and to the first sitting posture of the ritual prayer.

qalb: Heart. The human heart is the place of constant change and fluctuation. It is the suprarational organ of intuition where the Transcendent Realities enter into contact with man. The heart is the isthmus between this world and the next. The battlefield of the Greater Holy War is the heart. This is where the downward-pulling lower self is confronted by the yearning spirit. The battle is fought between these two adversaries in order for one to take possession of the precious heart of man. Under the misguidance of the Misguider, the lower self wants the heart to plummet to the depths of ignorance. However, the spirit, which is from Allah, exerts a powerful attraction upon the heart, as it endeavours to guide it towards Knowledge of Allah. The greater the purification of the heart the more receptive it is to this irresistible attraction of the celestial spirit. The heart is the sanctified centre of man because it is the place which contains Allah. Keeping watch over the heart is part of the Spiritual struggle of the Journey of Return. Those well advanced along the Path never allow any intruders to enter their sanctified hearts. The heart of the Perfect Man is the Divine Throne around which circle the spiritual realities.

rakat: One cycle of prayer. Each *rakat* is made up of seven movements.

ruh: Spirit. The *ruh* is that centre within man which is attracted and drawn back to its Source. The spirit endeavours to pull the heart towards Allah, while the lower self exerts a downward pull on the heart. The human spirit is also Allah's Spirit because Allah breathed His Spirit into man. In being both uncreated and created, the *ruh* makes its descent. On the Night of Power, "therein descend the angels and the Spirit, by Allah's permission" (Holy Qur'an 97:4). The uncreated spirit is equated with the Reality of Muhammad ﷺ and the created spirit extends from the Divine Throne down to the Perfect Man. The *ruh* cannot be seen except by the man who has outstripped "both the worlds." The spirit is neither within nor without the body, neither detached from it nor attached to it. It is both within and without, detached and attached. The luminosity which radiates from a man depends upon the degree of activity of his *ruh*.

safa: Purity. The higher teaching is Purity. The word Sufi derives from *safa*. The Sufi is the slave of Allah whose self, heart, spirit, and secret have been purified, through the Remembrance of Allah, through sincere spiritual endeavour and ultimately by Allah's Grace. His heart has become the dwelling place of Allah. He is the perfect locus of manifestation for the All-Comprehensive Name "Allah." An indication to the purification of the self from the human qualities.

salat: Prayer. It refers particularly to the ritual prayer. It is a connection between the slave and his Lord. The ritual ablution which precedes the *salat* symbolizes the separation from the self. The *salat* itself symbolizes the joining to Allah. The seven bodily postures of the ritual prayer are symbols of the stages on the Spiritual Journey of return to the Source and also the seven levels of knowledge through which the traveller (*salik*) passes on his ascent. As "the one who performs the prayer" (*musalli*) approaches closer to Allah, the more profound and intense is his salat. The Holy Prophet Muhammad ﷺ said, "The prayer without you is better than seventy." As his heart is purified through Spiritual struggle and the remembrance of Allah, and as he journeys along the path of return, the traveller leaves his lower self behind. Initially the Divine Light radiates into the heart of the *musalli/salik*. Gradually this Light increases and spreads, and eventually, through the Infinite Grace of Allah, it infuses and permeates every atom of his being. Then does he pray a prayer which is without himself, because "none worships Allah but Allah."

sawm: Fasting.

shahadah: Testimony of Faith. The witnessing or testimony or word. The supreme witnessing that defines Unity is the Islamic Testimony of Faith (*shahadah*). The *shahadah*, or declaration of faith, is *la ilaha il Allah, Muhammadan Rasul Allah* (there is no god other than Allah, and Muhammad is the Messenger of Allah). This declaration, witnessed by two people, marks a person's entry into Islam.

shari'ah: Sacred Law. *Shari'ah* makes manifest the Divine Reality (*haqiqa*). It provides all the principles and means for a human to develop true knowledge and acquire the noble character traits. Those who know Allah never leave His Sacred Law. Their courtesy towards Allah preserves them from letting the Scale of the Law slip from their hands.

shaykh: The Spiritual Master. He is the authentic guide and the only one to whom a seeker of Truth should turn in his quest. In turning to the Spiritual Master, the seeker is turning to Allah Almighty.

shaytaan: Satan represents the base faculties. He is lurking within the lower self and constantly trying to pull man downwards, away from the Divine. The Greater Holy War is waged against all lower tendencies.

silsilat: Spiritual chain. The spiritual chain of each *tariqa* descends from the Holy Prophet Muhammad himself ﷺ down to the present-day Shaykh. It is through his attachment to the *silsilat* that the newly initiated *murid* has the means to travel to Allah under Divine Protection.

suhoor: Pre-sunrise meal.

sunnah: Practice of the Holy Prophet ﷺ. The profound science of beautiful moral behaviour based upon the beautiful model of the Holy Prophet Muhammad ﷺ. Following the form of, and contemplating the meaning within, the sunnah are the most profound ways in which man can prepare himself to receive Divine Knowledge.

tariqa: Path. It is the narrow and steep Spiritual Path to Reality. The qualified seeker can travel this path only under the direction of a qualified Spiritual Guide. The name *tariqa* is specific to the Islamic Spiritual Path.

tasawwuf: Higher Teaching. Also known as the science of the self, *tasawwuf* is based upon the teachings of the Holy Prophet Muhammad ﷺ. It is known in the West as Sufism or Islamic mysticism. *Tasawwuf* is the acquisition of the noble character traits through purification of the heart, and is based on four foundations - Returning to Allah, asking forgiveness, developing spiritual consciousness, and good actions (*tauba, istighfaar, taqwa,* and *amal-salih*). The one who aspires to Knowledge of Allah is called a *mutasawwif.* The purified one who has made the journey of return, from his lower self to his higher-self, is a *Sufi.* The perfect *Sufi,* who is unknown to others, is from the people of blame. The master of the people of blame, the *Sufis,* the ones who aspire, the believers and the non-believers, is the Holy Prophet

Muhammad ﷺ. *Tasawwuf* is the science which takes the traveller through the unending degrees of knowing Allah. Our Master Muhammad ﷺ, the Chosen One, is the means by which his followers, lovers, and slaves may attain to Allah Almighty. *Tasawwuf* is spiritual and moral courtesy (*adab*). To every time, there are manners and to every state there are manners. Whoever holds fast to the higher ethics of all his times, will reach the higher place of the People of Allah. The one who sees the generosity of Allah upon him in every state, has the glad tidings that he will not follow the path of destruction. The manifestation of good manners outwardly is an indication to good manners inwardly as the Holy Prophet ﷺ said, "If his heart is in a state of submission then his limbs will follow suit." Whoever loses his good manners, is far away even though he may think he is near. He has been turned back from the same way that he thinks acceptance is taking place.

zakat: Compulsory tax.